Incredible Arachnids

John Townsend

Chicago, Illinois

For information, address the publisher:
Raintree, 100 N. LaSalle, Suite 1200, Chicago, IL 60602
Printed and bound in China
09 08 07 06 05
10 9 8 7 6 5 4 3 2 1

Library of Congress Cataloging-in-Publication Data

Townsend, John, 1955-
  Incredible arachnids / John Townsend.
     p. cm. -- (Incredible creatures)
  Includes bibliographical references (p.   ).
  Contents: Meet the family -- Amazing bodies -- Feeding -- Breeding -- Defense --
-- Weird and wonderful -- Arachnids in danger
  ISBN 1-4109-0526-8 (lib. bdg.-hardcover) -- ISBN 1-4109-0850-X (pbk.)
  1. Arachnida--Juvenile literature. [1. Spiders.] I. Title. II.
Series: Townsend, John, 1955- Incredible creatures.
  QL452.2.T68 2004
  595.4--dc22
                          2003019318

Acknowledgments
The publishers would like to thank the following for permission to reproduce photographs: pp. 4, 18 (left) Photodisc; pp. 5, 5 (top), 5 (middle), 6–7, 7, 8, 9 (right), 10, 11 (left), 12 (left), 13, 15 (right), 17, 19, 21 (left), 20, 22–23, 23, 24 (right), 26–27, 27, 28, 29 (right), 33 (left), 34–35, 35 (bottom), 38, 40, 43 (right), 45 (left), 45 (right), 46 (left), 48–49, 50–51 NHPA; pp. 5 (bottom), 14, 22 Sinclair Stammers/Science Photo Library; p. 6 Susumu Nishinaga/Science Photo Library; p. 9 (left), 38 Oxford Scientific Films; pp. 11 (right), 15 (left), 18 (right), 21 (right), 24 (left), 25, 26, 31 (left), 33 (right), 36 (right), 37, 39, 41, 44 (right), 46–47 FLPA; p. 12 Eye of Science/Science Photo Library; p. 16 David A. Northcott/Corbis; pp. 16–17 Galen Rowell/Corbis; p. 29 (left) Claude Nuridsany & Marie Perennou/Science Photo Library; p. 30 John Cancalosi/Nature Photo Library; pp. 31 (right), 40–41 Rod Preston-Mafham/Premaphotos Wildlife; p. 32 John S. Reid/California Academy of Science; p. 35 Ant Photo Library; p. 36 (left) Dr. Jeremy Burgess/Science Photo Library; p. 42 Andrew Syred/Science Photo Library; p. 43 (left) Dr. P. Marazzi/Science Photo Library; p. 48 Heather Angel/Natural Visions; p. 50 Rosenfeld Images Ltd./Science Photo Library; p. 51 Image Bank/Getty Images.

Cover photograph of a type of jumping spider reproduced with permission of Minden Pictures/FLPA.

Every effort has been made to contact copyright holders of any material reproduced in this book. Any omissions will be rectified in subsequent printings if notice is given to the publishers.

The publishers would like to thank Mark Rosenthal and Jon Pearce for their assistance in the preparation of this book.

Disclaimer
All the Internet addresses (URLs) given in this book were valid at the time of going to press. However, due to the dynamic nature of the Internet, some addresses may have changed, or sites may have changed or ceased to exist since publication. While the author and publishers regret any inconvenience this may cause readers, no responsibility for any such changes can be accepted by either the author or the publishers.

The paper used to print this book comes from sustainable resources.

Contents

Some words are shown in **bold.** You can find out what they mean by looking in the glossary. You can also look out for them in the "Wild Words" bank at the bottom of each page.

Amazing Arachnids!

Can you believe it?

The largest arachnids are tropical scorpions from India and West Africa. Some are 9.8 in. (25 cm) long. Even so, some spiders can measure more than 9.8 in. when they are stretched out. One could cover the front of this book.

Arachnids are all around us . . . hiding and waiting. Maybe that is why many people find them so scary. People shiver at the very thought of a hairy spider crawling over them.

Arachnids belong to a special group called **arthropods.** These are animals that have:
• a harder outside than the inside—the skeleton is inside out;
• a body with joints;
• and several legs with joints.

All **crustaceans,** such as crabs and lobsters, are arthropods. In fact, more than one million arthropods have been named so far. Some scientists think we know less than half of them. The rain forests alone may have millions more arthropods that we have never identified. Among all those unknown arthropods, there will be many mystery arachnids. A few may be near you right now!

abdomen   part of the body containing the stomach (the rear part of a spider)
arthropod   animal with jointed legs but no backbone

What are arachnids?

All arachnids have some things in common.
- They have eight legs.
- They have no backbone. This means they are **invertebrates.**
- Their bodies have two parts. The front part has sense **organs** and a pair of poison fangs. The back part has the **abdomen.** Sometimes these two parts are split by a thin waist. Sometimes they are joined together in one shell.

Nearly all arachnids:
- kill and eat other animals;
- live on dry land;
- and live on their own.

Arachnids are **vital** in the balance of nature. They control huge numbers of insects that harm plants, animals, and humans. We need arachnids. Even so, many people dread seeing them. **Arachnophobia** is the fear of spiders. Read on—if you dare!

▲ This rose tarantula is from Chile in South America.

Find out later . . .

Which arachnid has fangs like these?

Which arachnid has the deadliest bite?

Which arachnid can drink your blood?

---

crustacean sea arthropod with a hard shell, such as a crab, shrimp, or lobster
invertebrate animal without a backbone

Meet the Family

The arachnid family includes some amazing creatures, including spiders, scorpions, ticks, and mites.

Claws

Spiders' feet have two or three small claws that are used for climbing. Tiny hairs on these claws stick to surfaces and let the spiders walk on smooth or **vertical** surfaces—even upside down on glass. Their claws also cling on to the fine silk strands of their webs.

claws

Spiders

Spiders are found on land all over the world. They live in all **habitats,** even high in mountains. In fact, there are more than 40,000 different **species** of spider.

Spiders are not insects. They have a different type of body from insects. Like all arachnids, a spider has two parts to its body. The first is its head and **thorax** joined together. The second is its **abdomen** with the heart, gut, and lungs inside.

Spiders usually have eight legs and eight eyes. Unlike insects, they do not have **antennae** or wings. Scientists often put spiders into two types: web spiders that make webs to catch **prey,** and ground spiders that hunt their prey directly. Almost all spiders use poison to kill or **paralyze** their prey or to defend themselves.

antennae   feelers on an insect's head
habitat   natural home of an animal

Special tricks

- A thin shell called an exoskeleton covers a spider's body. As a spider grows, it has to **shed** this covering and grow a new one.
- When a spider catches prey, it uses a tiny pair of **pincers**. These are like hooked knives in front of its mouth. It uses these like hands, to dig or to carry. Each pincer has a sharp fang that can flick out to stab into the **victim.** Near the tip of the fang is a supply of poison. The fang acts like a needle to inject this **venom.** All spiders have these, but very few can **pierce** human skin. Even if they did, their poison would usually be too weak to cause any harm.

Number of known species in the top six spider families

Jumping spiders: 4,809
Sheet-web weavers
  and dwarf spiders:
  4,129
Orb weavers: 2,789
Wolf spiders: 2,245
Cobweb weavers:
  2,200
Crab spiders: 2,007

▼ Hairs on each of the spider's eight legs detect any movement nearby.

▲ Jumping spiders leap through the air to catch prey.

shed   get rid of an outer layer
thorax   part of the body between the head and abdomen; like a human's chest

Scorpion fact file

Size: Normally between 1.2–7.9 in. (3–20 cm) long

Life span: 3–5 years, some can live 10–15 years

Longest lived: 24 years

Distribution: Found almost everywhere except the North and South poles

Most are found in tropical and dry regions.

Scorpions and their bodies

There are almost 1,300 **species** of scorpion around the world. Many of them live in deserts. Some live in forests and in caves. They live in all continents except Antarctica.

All scorpions have powerful **pincers** to grab and rip up **prey**. These are like a spider's mouth parts, but much bigger. A scorpion also has extra eyes—often twelve in total. It has one central pair and three to five pairs of smaller eyes. These are just simple eyes, which sense light and dark. They do not see images in the way that insects, which have more complex eyes, can. This does not matter, because scorpions are mainly **nocturnal**. In fact, scorpions are covered with tiny hairs that detect the slightest air and ground movements. This means that they always know what is coming toward them.

▲ A cockroach makes a tasty snack for a scorpion.

gland   part of the body that makes chemicals and other substances
nocturnal   active at night and not in the day

Special features

The scorpion has more body **segments** than any other arachnid. It has many joints along its body. The **abdomen** has twelve segments, with the last five forming the "tail." The last segment is the **telson,** which has a bulb shape on the end. This contains the **venom glands** and has a sharp, curved stinger to inject the poison. It whips over the scorpion's head to strike at its prey or enemy.

The scorpion's underside has two sense **organs,** which seem to "sniff" chemicals left by other animals. These help it to find prey and other scorpions. Like spiders, scorpions **shed** their skin. They **molt** an average of five times before they are fully grown.

Scorpions in Arizona

At least 30 species of scorpion can be found in Arizona. Sometimes people get stung when they disturb them. If a scorpion feels under threat, its telson strikes. Most "stingings" happen at night during the warm summer months, but it is rare for anyone to get seriously sick.

▲ Scorpions wriggle free of their skins and often leave them in one piece.

This scorpion with its telson is ready to sting!

segment   section
species   type of living animal or plant

Extended family

Arachnids belong to a big class of **arthropods.** There are many smaller animals with a lot of the same features as spiders and scorpions.

Harvestmen

Harvestmen are related to true spiders, but they are different in that their **abdomen** and **thorax** are not separated by a waist and their body is not split into two parts. Harvestmen feed on small insects and other spiders. They are found everywhere from the Arctic to the tropics. They have very long, thin legs and a small body. They are sometimes called daddy longlegs. However, this name is more often used for the crane fly, which has long legs and wings. There are about 4,500 **species** of harvestmen around the world. Only a few of these will bite people.

Killers

Some harvestmen can have a **leg span** of 7.9 in. (20 cm). They are very quick. This helps them to kill and eat dangerous spiders, such as the deadly redback spider. People used to think harvestmen must have deadly **venom** as well. This is not true. They are just quicker than their **prey,** not more **venomous.**

▶ Harvestmen feed on plant juices or small insects.

leg span   distance between stretched-out legs
pincer   hook at the front of some creatures' mouths for holding food

Sun spiders

As you might expect, sun spiders tend to live in sunny places. They are active in the day, in full sunlight. They have big **pincers** and run very fast, so they often look like tiny scorpions being blown across the sand. That is why they are also called wind scorpions.

There are about 900 species of sun spider. Most are found in hot, dry areas in India, the Caribbean, the western United States, and northern Mexico. However, there are also many species of sun spider in Europe. They are like true spiders, but they have much bigger jaws, which stick out more. They use only their last three pairs of legs for running. Their front pair is used more like feelers. Sun spiders catch and feed on insects. They use their claws to tear them apart.

▲ This sun spider lives in the Kalahari Desert in Africa.

Mini scorpions

False scorpions, like the one above, are small arachnids that are only about 0.12–0.16 in. (3–4 mm) long. They are related to the true scorpions, spiders, and mites. They have claws, but because they lack the stinging tail of true scorpions, they are harmless. They mimic (act like) scorpions to fool other animals into thinking they are poisonous. There are about 2,000 species.

prey   animal that is killed and eaten
venomous   poisonous

Holding tight

The adult tick (shown below) has a tough skin and four pairs of clawed legs. Its mouth has a hook covered with more backward-curving hooks, so it cannot be pulled out of its host. It also makes a sort of cement that keeps it firmly stuck to its host's skin. It clings tight, even underwater.

Mites and ticks

Ticks and mites also belong to the arachnid family. There could be from 25,000 to 50,000 **species** of mite across the world. There could well be millions of one species living in the area around you right now.

Mites have their head, **thorax,** and **abdomen** all joined together in one body. They do not have a waist like spiders, but they do have the same number of legs. In fact, as mites are growing up, they often have just three pairs of legs and grow their extra pair as an adult. Some mites are just 0.008 in. (0.2 mm) long—they are **microscopic.** But this does not stop them from living on you, biting, and even spreading diseases.

► Mites even live on other arachnids. This one is feeding off a harvestman.

allergic   having a bad reaction, often involving sneezing, itching, or rashes
asthma   disease or allergic reaction that affects the lungs and breathing

Ticks

Ticks are **parasites** that need to live on a **host**. They choose an animal or a human to sink their mouth into and then drink its blood. Ticks are found in most parts of the world, but they prefer places with many animals around. Then they have more chance of feeding. Woods, tall grass, and shrubs are just right. They simply climb onto a leaf and wait to jump on a passing host.

Ticks are actually a type of mite and share many features with other mites. They are only small, from about 0.08–0.24 in. (2–6 mm) in length. Some females may reach 0.4 in. (1 cm) or more in diameter when they fill up with blood.

Did you know?

- Many people with **asthma** have the dust mite to blame. It is not dust or the mite itself to which these people are **allergic**. It is the mites' powdery droppings, which float in the air.

- In the United States, more than 20 million people have had asthma attacks. Mites are not always to blame, but they certainly have a major part to play.

- About 17 million people in the United States, 3.5 million people in the United Kingdom, and 2 million people in Australia have asthma.

◀ Dust mites smaller than 0.02 in. (0.4 mm) float in the air with dust.

>>>>>>>>>>

Find out more about mites and disease on page 42.

host   animal or plant that has a parasite living in or on it
parasite   animal or plant that lives in or on another living thing

Amazing Bodies

Ancient scorpions

Scorpions breathe with book lungs. Their ancestors may have come out of the sea 440 million years ago. Scientists have found **fossil** scorpions like the one below. They were up to 3.3 ft (1 m) long and had **gills** instead of lungs, showing that they lived in water.

If you open a book and let the pages fan apart, you will get an idea of what an arachnid's lungs look like. In fact, they are called book lungs because there are layers of air between the "pages" of **tissue**. Spiders have either two or four book lungs. The blood absorbs **oxygen** from the air that is breathed in.

Breathing

Narrow slits under a spider's **abdomen** lead to the book lungs. But a spider also breathes through a network of tubes that runs all around its body. As air flows through these, the oxygen gets into the blood and to all the **organs**. With this backup system of breathing, spiders are not likely to get out of breath very often.

Blood and water

Spider blood is light blue. It is pumped by a heart that is a different shape from our hearts. A spider's heart is long, like a tube. The blood travels to the book lungs, where it releases **carbon dioxide** and picks up a fresh supply of oxygen before going around the body again.

Spiders need air. Most quickly drown in water. But one spider lives underwater. The water spider builds a silk air bubble underwater, among plants. It is a good swimmer and catches **prey** by stunning it with **venom.** It then takes its meal back home to the air-filled den. The spider swims from the den to the surface when it needs more oxygen. It collects air on its furry abdomen so it can take oxygen down to its underwater home.

carbon dioxide gas that animals and humans breathe out
gills flaps on the sides of a fish's head used for breathing oxygen from water

Breathing mites

Many mites take in air from all over their body surface. They also have a system of tubes to carry air through their bodies. Although mites must breathe air, their small bodies do not need much oxygen. Many mites can stay underwater for a long time, as shown below.

▲ This is a water spider with its life-saving air bubble.

oxygen   one of the gases in air and water that all living things need
tissue   soft parts of the body; a collection of cells

Surviving

Like all animals, arachnids can only **survive** with a regular supply of **oxygen** and food. Wherever they happen to live, arachnids must adapt to make full use of their surroundings. Sometimes it is not easy to find oxygen and food.

Scorpions can survive in the harshest **climates.** Some go without food for up to a year. This is because they can eat a huge amount in one sitting. They also burn up energy at a slow rate, so they need less food to survive. It is the same with oxygen. Scorpions have even been found under snow-covered rocks over 13,100 ft (4,000 m) high in the Andes Mountains. This is so high up that the air is thin, but the scorpions can still survive.

Hot and cold

Scorpions have to be tough. Deserts are blistering hot in the day and can drop below freezing at night. Scorpions can survive being cooled to below freezing. They can cope with a huge range in temperature.

▶ The summit of Mount Everest is 29,029 ft (8,848 m) above sea level. Not far below, arachnids live in this icy world.

climate   general weather conditions in an area over a period of time
inhabitant   person who lives in a certain place

High-living

When climbers were trying to get to the top of Mount Everest in the 1920s, they were amazed to find spiders alive at more than 22,950 ft (7,000 m). Tiny black attid spiders are the highest **inhabitants** of Earth. Even mountain goats cannot breathe and eat at heights of more than 16,400 ft (5,000 m). The spiders live in small cracks in the rock and ice. Not only is it bitterly cold, but there is hardly any oxygen. It is good that spiders have two ways to get air into their bodies. Food is very rare at such a height, too. These spiders are real survivors.

Dry as dust

Scorpions get all the water they need from the insects they eat. They keep all the water inside their watertight bodies. No water is lost: the scorpion's body uses every drop. Its waste is just a dry powder.

Feeding

The web site

Spiders spend a lot of time waiting. As soon as they feel a slight tug on a thread, they strike. They rush out to kill . . . or to repair a broken web. Some spiders eat their old webs before starting a new one. Others just roll up the web and throw it away as a tiny silk ball.

Catching food is the spider's special skill. Not all spiders build webs, but all can make silk from **glands** on their **abdomen.** Many spiders lay out a line of dry silk behind them as they move around. This dragline acts as a safety line, like a mountain climber's rope. Other glands make **cocoon** threads for wrapping up the spider's eggs.

Spiders' silk threads are very thin, but they are as strong as a nylon thread. Spider threads are tough and elastic enough to withstand the impact of a flying insect. The bolas spider leaves a drop of liquid silk on its web. This has a chemical in it that attracts male moths. They fly into it and get caught in the sticky blob. The spider's dinner is served.

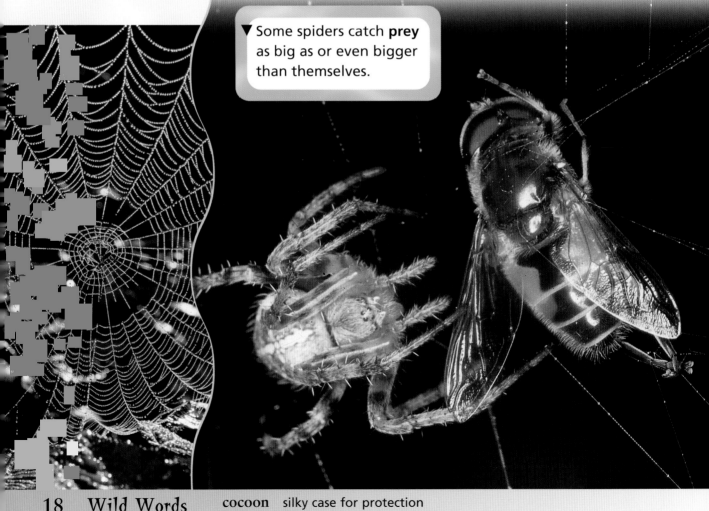

▼ Some spiders catch **prey** as big as or even bigger than themselves.

cocoon   silky case for protection
funnel   cone shape

Web design

Spiders' webs come in all shapes and sizes. Some spiders build **irregular,** flimsy webs while others seem to create great designs. Common house spiders make their webs into a **funnel** with a den in the end, where they can hide and wait.

Cobweb spiders build a silk mesh with sticky threads. Insects soon get stuck, and the more they struggle, the more they become tangled. Many spider webs are found near the ground, although some span wide-open spaces between bushes or trees. Many spiders have bad eyesight and build webs at night by relying on their sense of touch. They then wait for breakfast to arrive.

FAST FACTS

The web of an average European garden spider contains 66–98 ft (20–30 m) of silk, but weighs less than 0.00002 oz (0.5 mg).

◄ This spider is releasing silk from its abdomen.

irregular   no organized pattern, shape, or design

Spit and chew

Some spiders spit. When they creep up on their prey, they spit a mixture of **venom** and glue at it. This quickly "freezes" their target. The spider can then feed on a fresh, live dinner that does not wiggle too much.

FAST FACTS

Orb web spiders spin some of the largest webs, up to 6.6 ft (2 m) across, which can catch small birds and bats.

Finding food

Carnivores have a harder job finding food than plant-eaters. After all, their food not only moves around, but it can also run away. Many arachnids have learned to sit and wait. This way, they save energy by letting their food come to them. Otherwise, they could spend all day searching and finding nothing.

Most scorpions get their food by sitting quietly at the entrance to their **burrow** and waiting for something to walk by. Other scorpions are more active hunters and wander around looking for food. They hold their claws wide open, ready to spring shut on any **prey** that bumps into them.

▲ This spitting spider has caught a mosquito.

carnivore   animal that eats meat
mange   skin disease causing itching and loss of hair in animals

Good eyes

Zebra spiders do not need to make webs and wait. They are thought to have the best eyesight of any **arthropod.** If you take a close look at one of these spiders, it will often turn its head to look straight back at you.

These spiders use their large front eyes to find and **stalk** their prey. Using their good eyesight, they are able to judge distance well. That means they can jump and hit their target. Before jumping, they glue a silk thread to the surface from which they are jumping. If they miss the target, they can climb up the thread and try again. They ignore ants, so maybe ants do not taste very good.

▲ A zebra spider's large eyes will often stare straight at you.

Hungry pests

Most mites feed on the bodies or blood of larger animals, like the ones on a beetle above. Some mites carry diseases like **mange** or **scabies,** which they give to their **host** when they bite. Some plant mites are major pests of farmers' crops. A few **species** of mite are pests in stored food such as flour, yeast, cheese, or powdered milk.

scabies   skin disease causing severe itching
stalk   hunt down by following and creeping up on a victim

Danger

There are hundreds of types of tick, but few affect humans and pets. Even so, if you find a tick on your skin, it is wise to see a doctor. Ticks can spread Lyme disease, which can sometimes kill people. Only five people in 100,000 catch it in the United States. But this ratio is much higher in Connecticut, where more than 125 people in 100,000 catch the disease each year.

Sucking blood

Ticks also spend a lot of time waiting around. A path used by sheep is a good place to sit and wait. The tick gets ready when it senses **carbon dioxide** and movement. These are signals that a possible **host** is nearby. The tick crawls onto the animal and clings onto it with its front legs. Then it finds a safe spot where it will not be rubbed off. It sinks its sharp **pincers** into the host's skin and hooks itself on. It slowly sucks up blood. Its tiny body starts to swell up like a pea. When it is full, the tick lets go and drops off again. Now the tick may **molt** or lay eggs. Or it might just wait for the next host to come along.

disinfectant   liquid or ointment that kills germs

Thirsty

There are four stages to a tick's life. The first is the egg, which hatches into a **larva** with six legs. It can suck blood and usually finds a small host like a mouse, lizard, or bird. The larva feeds, grows, and molts to become a **nymph** with eight legs. The deer tick is about the size of a pinhead in its nymph stage, while the common dog tick is slightly bigger. The tick is still not a full adult until it feeds again and molts. Only now does it become either a male or female that can mate. The adult female requires a blood meal before she lays her eggs. Deer, sheep, cattle, dogs, cats, and humans make perfect hosts.

▼ After filling up with blood, the female tick is ready to lay her eggs.

Taking off a tick

If you find that a tick has bitten you or your pet, it is important to remove it correctly. Use fine-point tweezers to grasp the tick as close to the skin as possible. With a slow, smooth motion, pull firmly and steadily outward and do not twist or squeeze the tick. Clean the wound with **disinfectant**.

larva   young form of an animal that is very different from the adult
nymph   in-between stage from larva to adult

Eating mom

Many female spiders die soon after laying their eggs. The hatching baby spiders, like the ones below, do not let fresh meat go to waste. Their first meal is their own mother.

▲ Baby spiders hatching.

Digestion

Scorpions sense when **prey** is nearby from **vibrations** in the air and ground. To kill the prey, a scorpion seizes it in its **pincers** and injects **venom** with its tail. This will either kill the prey in seconds or **paralyze** it. A large scorpion may just rip the prey up into bits.

Eating is more of a problem. A scorpion can only eat liquid food. It has to break up the prey's skeleton and spit **digestive juices** onto it to turn the victim's insides into a soup. Some scorpions shred their prey, put the bits into a space just below their front legs, and spit in digestive juices. They wait until the prey's **tissues** become like jelly and then suck up the fluids.

▲ A black scorpion quickly kills a gecko in the Sahara.

cell   tiny building block that makes up all living things
filter   something that traps large bits

Spider food

A spider's digestion is like a scorpion's because it begins outside its body. When a spider catches an insect, it stabs it with its fangs and injects venom into the wound. This will paralyze the prey before it kills it. The spider then **regurgitates** juices into the wound to break down the insect's body tissue and turn it to liquid. A spider cannot eat solid food—it can only slurp liquid and paste. Muscles suck the soup through the spider's mouth and into the stomach. Two **filters** in the mouth stop bits of solid food from getting into the digestive system. **Nutrients** are absorbed as the spider takes a nap.

Many mites

Mites eat many different kinds of food. Some **species** suck juice from plants, some eat fungi, and some feed on other small animals. Some eat **cells** growing in water. Every type of animal has mite **parasites,** except for fish.

◄ These red spider mites are highly magnified. Each one is really less than 0.04 in. (1 mm) long. The leaves they live on get covered with fine webs and yellow spots.

nutrient   important substance found in food and needed by the body
vibration   quivering movement or fast shaking

25

Breeding

When two scorpions meet, they usually fight until one is killed and eaten by the winner. That can make mating rather dangerous. Most scorpions do not interact with others because they end up trying to eat each other. Since females are usually bigger than their mates, it is often the male that turns into dinner.

Meeting

The male scorpion has a courtship display to make sure the female knows he is not on the menu. Some males tend to rock and shake. Some might sting the female. Others hit the female with their tail. Males tend to have much longer tails than females, so these may be more important for impressing a mate than for hunting. In fact, a male has to try anything to take his mate's mind off killing him.

Unfair!

Most spiders live only one or two years. However, large female tarantulas can live for up to twenty years. Male tarantulas live only two or three years. Many male spiders die soon after mating.

▼ The male scorpion, on the right, tries to mate and make a quick getaway.

fertilize   when a sperm joins an egg to make a new individual

Mating spiders

Finding the right female can be tricky for a male spider. Luckily, a female spider leaves chemicals in the air or on her silk threads, like a perfume. They tell any passing male that she is on the lookout for a mate. But a male spider has to prove himself to her. A female will only accept a male who performs a type of dance. This tells her if he is the right **species.**

If she is satisfied with the male, the female spider lets him transfer his **sperm** into her. She may keep the sperm inside her for months before it **fertilizes** her eggs. She lays the eggs in a silky **cocoon** and usually has nothing more to do with them.

Parting

Despite the stories, the female black widow spider does not usually kill her partner after mating. In some species, a female may mate only once. In other species, the female may mate with several males during her lifetime. Sometimes females kill the males, but with most spiders, both sexes part peacefully after mating.

▲ The male wolf spider is smaller than the female.

sperm   male sex cell

Water mites

Most water mites lay eggs wrapped up inside small blobs of jelly. They stick these to plant stems, the lower surface of leaves, or the underside of floating plants. A few **species** of water mite do not lay eggs, but give birth to live young.

▶ Water mites swim to a place to lay their eggs.

Nests and birth

Scorpions are among the few **arthropods** that do not lay eggs. Some females can store **sperm** from the male in their bodies until they are ready to **fertilize** their eggs. The fertilized eggs then develop inside their bodies. It can take from several months to over a year before the young are born.

Special features

Some baby scorpions are fully formed when they are born, even though their skin stays white and soft until the second time they **molt.** Others look like fat, white maggots with tiny **pincers.** They only look like scorpions after they molt for a second time. Then they change shape and their shell turns dark and hard. Being a young scorpion is not easy. There are plenty of **predators** out there waiting for a quick bite.

egg sac   small case that holds an egg or eggs and food for the young to eat

Dinner date

The female nursery web spider gets hungry and may eat her mate. To make her less likely to attack him, the male wraps up an insect and gives it to her as a sort of gift. While she is busy eating her meal, he mates with her. The mating lasts for about an hour, until the female has finished eating her gift. Then the male runs off, never to be seen by her again.

The female makes an **egg sac,** which she carries around with her in her jaws. When the eggs are ready to hatch, she makes a "nursery web," like a little tent, to protect her young. She will stay on guard to fight off any predators.

Leaving the nest

Many spiders' nests are bundles of silk and are often high in bushes or trees. Tiny spiders hatch out of the nest and have to go off into the world. They just leap from the nest attached by their silk draglines, as shown below. It looks like a group of bungee jumpers all leaping at once. This is called ballooning.

▲ This female nursery web spider is watching over her nest.

molt   lose skin or hair before new growth
predator   animal that hunts and eats other animals

Staying together

A mother emperor scorpion provides food for her young while they grow up as a family. The young also share their mother's **burrow**. Some emperor scorpions build spaces inside termite mounds and live together in a group or **hibernate** together in the winter.

Parents

Male arachnids have nothing to do with rearing young. Some females leave their young to fend for themselves. Others guard them, feed them, or carry them around.

Some mother scorpions keep their babies on their backs for about a week. Most of these mothers form a "birth basket" with their **pincers** to catch the babies as they are born. The babies then climb onto their mother's back. They die if they fall off. Soon after their first **molt,** the babies jump from their mother's back and can feed on their own. But sometimes, they stay on their mother as long as they can until after their second molt, feeding off the remains of their mother's meals.

▶ A female emperor scorpion carries her young.

abandon   give up and leave something behind
hibernate   "close down" the body to rest when it is too cold or dry

Mother spiders

Most female spiders lay several hundred eggs. Some of the larger wolf spiders can lay thousands in just a few minutes. All spiders spin a **cocoon** as a case for the developing eggs. Many females **abandon** their cocoon as soon as they have made it. Usually, they hide the cocoon away in a crack or under leaves, where it will be safe. Other mother spiders guard and defend their cocoon until the eggs hatch.

Female wolf spiders attach their cocoons to themselves and carry them around. Like scorpions, the young spiders climb onto their mother's back when they hatch. Hundreds of tiny spiders cover her back for about a week before they leave to **survive** on their own.

Mother care

Mothercare spiders are one of the few **species** of spider that look after their young once they have hatched. Despite her small size, the female can kill bees and wasps. She eats them and returns to her young. She feeds her young by **regurgitating** food into their mouths.

▼ A female mothercare spider looks after her young.

▲ A mother wolf spider provides a taxi service for her young.

regurgitate   throw up the contents of the stomach

Defense

Arachnids have their fair share of **venom.** While its main purpose is to kill and digest **prey,** venom can be very useful when a **predator** comes along. The predator is sure to leave the arachnid alone to avoid pain—or worse.

Arachnids have a range of venom strength. All scorpions and spiders have venom, but it is not always very strong. Also, their ability to inject depends on the size of their fangs or sting. Most venom is **toxic** to insects and sometimes to **mammals.** Scorpions with small, weak **pincers** tend to have stronger venom in their stings. Large scorpions may not sting, preferring to use their strong pincers for attack or defense.

Deadly

While the yellow fat-tailed scorpion is thought to cause the most human deaths, the death stalker has even stronger venom. This scorpion grows up to 3.9 in. (10 cm) in length and is sometimes called the Palestine yellow scorpion.

► The death stalker scorpion is found in North Africa and the Middle East.

antidote　medicine to make a poison safe
exaggerated　made to sound like a bigger deal than it is; far-fetched

Danger to humans

Scorpions tend to have a bad reputation for harming people. This danger is often **exaggerated.** After all, there are more than 1,000 types of scorpion, yet only 20 or so have venom that is dangerous to humans.

Only one of the United States' scorpions needs careful handling. The desert scorpion is found in Arizona, California, and southern Utah. To defend itself, it will sometimes sting a person. The venom can cause pain and swelling, numbness, foaming at the mouth, and muscle twitching. As with any venom, problems can occur if someone has an **allergic** reaction. Death is very rare. An **antidote** can cure severe cases. Even so, if you find one of these scorpions, it is best to leave it alone.

Estimates

No one really knows how many people scorpions kill because deaths do not get reported in **remote** desert areas. People in North Africa tell how a yellow fat-tailed scorpion (below) can kill a person in seven hours and a small dog in seven minutes. It is thought that this **species** may kill more than 250 people each year in Tunisia.

◀ Scientists collect scorpion venom to make an antidote to the sting.

remote   faraway place in the middle of nowhere
toxic   poisonous

Spider venom

Despite what some people may fear, spiders do not go on the prowl looking for a human to bite. The reason spiders have **venom** is to help them digest food. They always prefer to run away when disturbed, but sometimes they have no choice but to bite. If they happen to take shelter in an empty shoe and then a big foot steps in it, biting is their only defense.

The Brazilian wandering spider is yellow and is sometimes called the banana spider. In one bite it can inject 0.0002 oz (6 mg) of venom. Just 0.00004 oz (1 mg) could be a **lethal** amount for humans. This **species** of spider is feared in Brazil. There are reported cases of it killing young children.

▼ The banana spider is also called the golden silk spider. This female is many times bigger than the male below her.

lethal deadly
official record   information reported by the correct authority

Deadly?

The brown recluse spider is often called the violin spider because it has a dark violin-shape on its brown body. This is one of the six **venomous** spiders found in many states in the eastern United States. Its bite is painless until three to eight hours later. The wound then becomes **swollen** and tender. It is estimated that one or two people die from spider bites in the United States each year.

Australia is famous for spiders with strong venom. However, only the Sydney **funnel**-web and redback spiders have killed people. Records show fewer than 30 people have died in Australia from spider bites. None of these deaths happened in the last 20 years. About 200 redback spider bites need **antidote** treatment every year.

▲ The bite of the funnel-web spider can be treated with an antidote.

Tarantulas

Many people think the larger tarantulas like the one below are deadly, simply because they look scary. But a tarantula like the one below can only inject about 0.00005 oz (1.5 mg) of venom, and 0.0004 oz (12 mg) would be needed to kill a human. There are no **official records** of a human dying as the result of a tarantula bite.

swollen   puffed-up, enlarged
venom   poison

Vanishing act

- The giant crab spider can look just like tree bark. It can stretch out or squeeze up tight to fit in with its background.

- Orb-weaver spiders can stretch themselves out to hide on the stem of a plant. No passing predator is likely to take a second look.

Camouflage and color

Most arachnids are small and likely to be a tempting meal for reptiles such as snakes and birds with good eyesight. So the secret is to stay out of sight.

Tropical spiders that spend a lot of time on tree bark have excellent **camouflage**. They blend in so well with their surroundings that it is hard to see them, even close up. Hairs on spiders also help to "soften their edges" and stop them from making sharp, dark shadows.

The long-jawed orb spider has a great trick to **disguise** its nest. It leaves its **egg sac** on a grass stem for all to see. But it looks just like a bird dropping that has landed on the grass, so no one is likely to go near it.

▶ The orb spider works hard at disguising her egg sac.

▲ Crab spiders often look like part of the flower on which they live. This one is inside a poppy.

burrow   hole made for shelter; also, to make such a hole
camouflage   color that matches the background

Looks can save lives

Because they hide during the day and are mainly active at night, most scorpions do not need as clever camouflage as do some spiders. In the daytime, they hide in their **burrows** and cracks or hang under rocks and branches. Even so, those that live in deserts are often sandy-colored, so they are hard to see. Darker scorpions that live on the dark rain forest floor can be active in the shadows during the day.

If mites need to avoid a **predator's** sticky tongue, why are some so brightly colored? Most predators know that bright colors, spots, and stripes on small animals are often warnings of poison or a bad taste. It is like a sign saying, "Don't bother, I taste disgusting."

Hard to see

- Trap-door spiders live in tiny holes. They make little flaps over their holes to hide under, just like trap doors.

- If you are a brightly colored spider, where can you hide? Simple: right in the middle of a flower petal of the same color.

◄ Sand wolf spiders look like speckled grains of sand. No bird will spot them from the sky.

disguise   change appearance to look different

Running on water

How useful it must be to walk over water. A few animals can do this, including the water mites shown below. They are very light and have hairy legs that trap air bubbles, so they can run across the surface of a pond. This is an excellent way to escape from something that wants to eat you.

Other tricks

Long-jawed orb spiders make their nests look like a bird dropping, but bird dropping spiders look like droppings themselves! This stops any **predators** from trying to carry them away. During the day, bird dropping spiders sit on leaves and pretend to be bird droppings. This not only hides them from predators, it also helps them to catch and trick insects.

Many spiders can get away quickly if they are under attack in a tree. They act just like Spider-man! They leap into the air on a silk thread and **rappel** out of danger.

mammal   warm-blooded animal that has hair and feeds its young with milk
pedipalps   spider's two feelers, like short front legs; used for touching and tasting

Keep off

When a predator threatens a large bird-eating spider, the spider just shakes. This throws its hairs into the face of the attacker. These hairs irritate the attacker when they get into its eyes and mouth. The spider then runs off—bald but safe.

The raft spider has a clever way of escaping. It has tiny waterproof hairs on its feet that trap air pockets. It can run over the surface of water to get away. The barking spider is an Australian tarantula, often called the whistling spider. When under attack, it makes a noise by rubbing its **pedipalps** over its fangs. This makes a whistling noise that is scary enough to make predators leave it alone.

Hiding makes sense

Not all scorpions are aggressive killers. Many **species** are very small and in constant danger from other animals. Although they have tiny stingers with **venom** to defend themselves, scorpions fall **prey** to all sorts of predators. Birds, centipedes, tarantulas, lizards, and **mammals** such as meerkats (below) will all kill scorpions.

◄ A raft spider often waits with two feet in the water. When it feels ripples from prey, it runs across the pond to attack.

Weird and Wonderful

Arachnids are not our favorite animals. People get upset when spiders or cobwebs appears in their homes during the winter. They would prefer that they stay outside like the many **species** of spider in Canada that stay active under the snow for up to six months. Temperatures there can range from 21 to 27 °F (–6 to –3 °C). The spiders may be able to **survive** by having a sort of **antifreeze** in their bodies. Scientists think that spiders may eat nectar from flowers to keep their **cells** from freezing. They fill up with sugar and become so "syrupy" they cannot freeze.

Perhaps people would welcome spiders into their homes if they thought about what spiders eat. Spiders help to get rid of dust mites, lice, and fleas that may sometimes hide in carpets.

Fear

Of the 40,000 species of spider, only about 30 species produce bites that may cause harm to humans. Yet more people are scared of spiders than any other small creature. Scientists think about 3 percent of people have an extreme fear of spiders. This is called **arachnophobia.** It can make some people freeze with fear.

antifreeze   liquid that does not freeze at temperatures below 32 °F (0 °C)
arachnophobia   fear of spiders

Black widows and grapes

In 2002 a woman got a shock in Massachusetts when she took a bunch of grapes from her bag and found a black widow spider inside. "We're seeing more of this kind of thing," a spider expert said. "We're using fewer **pesticides**, so the spiders are **thriving**. The black widow may strike fear in people, but its bad name is unfair. In 33 years, I can't recall anyone dying from a black widow bite."

A woman in Liverpool, England, also found a dead spider in her grapes. It was only when she threw away the spider that she realized its hourglass shape meant it was a black widow. Newspapers were full of the story, which set off fears of spiders once again.

◄ You can tell a black widow spider from the hourglass shape on it.

pesticide   poison sprayed onto crops to kill insects
thriving   growing with strength and doing very well

Arachnids to make you scratch

Bird mites infest the skin of birds. The chicken mite attacks domestic poultry and may also give humans a skin rash. But worst for us are **follicle** mites. They are only 0.01 in. (0.25 mm) long, and they get into hair follicles and sweat **glands.** When they bite, you scratch.

Itchy

There is a tiny mite that **burrows** into animals' skin and causes **scabies.** It feeds on skin **cells** and lays eggs in the **host's** skin. Three to four days after hatching, the **larvae** emerge. Then they find another area on the body where they **burrow** under the skin and lay their eggs. And so it goes on. In humans, these scabies mites cause a lot of itching. There is often a rash of **blisters.** Elderly people can be badly attacked by scabies mites.

Some mites are so tiny they live inside bees. They get into the bees' breathing tubes. Sometimes a whole hive of honey bees can be infected with these mites. Many beekeepers have problems controlling these arachnids that cannot be seen.

▲ Follicle mites like this often live in the eyelashes or ears of humans, without causing harm.

blister   small bubble or swelling on the skin
follicle   any small opening in the skin, such as a hair follicle

Chiggers

Harvest mites are bright red and can often be seen crawling over the soil. They look like small red spiders. They become a problem when they breed. In some areas, like the southern United States, these mites lay their eggs in the soil in the spring. The larvae that hatch are called chiggers. They are **microscopic** and suck fluids from our skin. Once a chigger has jumped on you, it will inject **venom** into the bite wound and suck up the **tissue** juices. The bite will itch for weeks. That is longer than the chigger is likely to live. There is something about the human **immune system** that stops the chigger from having a full feeding. At least that is a comfort as you scratch yourself to sleep.

Ticks

If you want to keep ticks (like the one below) off your skin, it is best to live near water. Scientists have noted that ticks tend to stay away from wet places. It is thought that ticks may not **survive** freezing if they are wet. They tend to spend the winter hiding under dry leaves. They "drink" by absorbing water from humid air.

▲ **Scabies** mites tunnel into the skin to lay eggs. Scratching only makes the skin sore.

immune system   body's natural defense against infection

Big

The biggest arachnids are usually harmless to humans. Black emperor scorpions are one of the biggest, but they are only as heavy as a chicken's egg. Some grow to 7.9 in. (20 cm) long and kill insects, small birds, and **mammals** in the forests of Africa. The black emperor's poison does not harm humans—it is like getting a bee sting. But that is enough to keep most animals away, apart from the baboon. Baboons like to eat scorpions for a snack. They just rip off the stinger and munch the rest.

Like all scorpions, the black emperor glows bright green or blue under **ultraviolet** light. Scientists are not really sure why. Perhaps insects can see them glow in the dark and are attracted to them. When they get close, the scorpion attacks. Scorpions may be like living bug zappers!

▶ This baboon is digging for scorpions in Africa.

protein   nutrient in food that is used by the body for growth and repair
ultraviolet   invisible light from the sun

Giant spiders

The Goliath bird-eating spider is the largest tarantula in the world. It lives in the tropical rain forests of South America. The female's **leg span** can reach more than 9.8 in. (25 cm) long, and she may weigh over 7 oz (200 g). The spider's fangs are 1 in. (2.5 cm) long and can stab a person's skin. But its **venom** is not too strong, and a bite will only cause mild swelling for a few hours.

Despite their name, these spiders do not often eat birds. Even so, they are large enough to catch the chicks of ground-nesting birds. They usually eat large insects, lizards, and frogs.

Female Goliath bird-eaters usually live from six to fourteen years, but males live only half this time. In fact, if the air is not damp enough when these spiders **molt,** they cannot **shed** their skin, and so they die.

▲ A tarantula stabs its victims with its fangs.

Tarantula facts

- Tarantulas may go without food for several months.

- They range from as small as a fingernail to as big as a dinner plate.

- They have tiny claws that can go in and out, just like a cat's.

- They will go bald on their **thorax** when they get old.

▲ This is a Goliath bird-eating spider.

Arachnids in Danger

Few left

The cream-colored tooth cave spider is in danger of becoming **extinct**. It is only about 0.6 in. (1.6 mm) long and lives in just a few caves in Texas. It has no natural **predators**, but many of the caves where it lives have been filled in or bricked-up. This rare spider may not survive without help.

For sale in Peru: dead spiders and butterflies from the rain forests.

As the human population of the world grows, many wild animals struggle to **survive**. Land is cleared and drained for farming, forests are cut down, and towns are built. The fine balance between living **species** can be upset. If one link in the **food chain** is broken, others will soon break down, too.

At risk

Like many wild animals, arachnids are under threat from poison. It can be put into their **habitat** on purpose when farmers spray the land to get rid of pests. Fumes, chemicals, and garbage also **pollute** our world.

Sun scorpions are at risk in British Columbia in Canada. Grassland has been plowed up to plant crops. **Pesticides** and cattle grazing have changed the natural habitat.

▲ Forest fires can destroy millions of arachnids in one day.

extinct   die out, never to return
food chain   order in which one living thing feeds on another

On the brink

The other threat to larger arachnids is trapping. People catch them in large numbers to sell as pets. Tarantulas and scorpions make big money for people all over the world.

Mexican red-kneed tarantulas are in danger. They have been caught in large numbers since the 1970s to be sold as pets. They are also killed because they happen to look scary. Red-kneed tarantulas have bright orange-red markings around the middle of each leg. This species is now protected and cannot be sold from Mexico or **imported** into the United States. The American Tarantula Society is now breeding these spiders in **captivity.**

Many people do care if these arachnids disappear forever. Protecting wild areas may save these species before it is too late.

CUSTOMS SEIZE RARE BUGS

Australia, 2000

An **endangered** tarantula and five endangered scorpions have been seized by **customs** after being found in mail at a Melbourne postal center. The attempt to import the African scorpions and a tarantula failed after a customs worker inspected a package from the United Kingdom. An official said, "Australia is determined to stamp out this **illegal** trade in wildlife."

FAST FACTS

The ladybird spider is one of the rarest in the United Kingdom. The males have a bright red back with four black spots.

import   bring into the country from another country
pollute   ruin natural things with dangerous chemicals, fumes, or garbage

> ► A yellow-billed hornbill enjoys a scorpion snack.

Mite snacks

Even though mites are pests, they are an important food source for many animals. Predators of mites include the following: ants, beetles, harvestmen, other mites, small spiders, small centipedes, small fish, small frogs, small toads, small birds, small lizards, and small salamanders.

cannibal   animal that eats its own species
endangered   in danger of dying out completely

Enemies

Arachnids do not just have problems with humans. It must seem like the whole world is against them. Despite a scorpion's armor and sting, many animals think it is worth a fight. Scorpions are a major source of fat, **nutrients,** and water for hungry animals, especially in dry areas. Some **predators** become immune to the **venom** of scorpions. After a while, a bird, bat, or lizard can **tolerate** amounts that would kill other animals. Even so, if stung with enough venom, they will still be at great risk. Some animals take that risk and attack the scorpion's stinger first. It is hardly surprising that most scorpions spend 80 percent of their time hiding in or near their safe **burrows.**

Spider snacks

Spiders have soft bodies and are a tasty meal for many predators. Birds, reptiles, and scorpions catch spiders from the ground or out of their webs. Some wasps **specialize** in spider hunting. Spider wasps inject their eggs into spiders' bodies. These eggs hatch and the **larvae** eat the spiders from inside. There are also spider flies that attack spiders and deposit the young fly larvae on their bodies. These burrow into the spider's book lungs and kill it.

The praying mantis eats any spider it runs into. But perhaps the greatest threat to spiders is other spiders. When food is rare, some spiders turn into **cannibals** and eat their own young. The chances of a spider reaching old age are not high.

The unknown

No mites are known to be **endangered,** but we do not know very much about most of them. Nobody seems to worry too much about mites being at risk. But some mites live on larger animals that are endangered, so if the **host species** becomes **extinct,** the mites may go, too. That could affect the whole **food chain.**

specialize   focus on one thing and be skilled at it
tolerate   put up with something

Scientists have been using scorpion **venom** to develop new drugs. They are using different venoms to help doctors perform **organ** transplants or treat diseases such as **arthritis.** One day, scorpion venom might be curing people instead of hurting them.

Arachnids and us

Arachnids are important to us all. Without them, our planet would be overrun with insects. Our crops and our health would suffer. On the other hand, some mites and ticks affect us by spreading disease and giving us **allergies.** They are responsible for millions of dollars' worth of farming losses each year.

Mites are everywhere—from our own beds to hot volcanic springs. They get into the skins of animals, under the shells of turtles, and into our own hair. We still do not know how many **species** of mites are out there. And not all mites are pests. They and their **larvae** feed thousands of other animals. They are a **vital** part of every **ecosystem.**

▶ These **funnel**-web spiders are having their venom taken to use as an **antidote** to their bite.

arthritis   painful disease affecting the joints of the body
ecosystem   balance between all living things in their natural environment

Spider farms

Humans have used spider silk for a long time. The ancient Romans sealed up wounds with spider silk—it is soft, strong, and free of germs. Spider silk can be woven into cloth. The Chinese gave Great Britain's Queen Victoria a spider silk gown in 1896. For many years, scientists have tried to make fibers as strong as spider thread. The study of spiders is still of great interest.

One of the challenges for the future is how we can manage to keep a healthy balance of different species. We must be careful that **pesticides** do not destroy all insects and arachnids forever. By learning more about arachnids, we may start to understand what part these incredible creatures play in the life of our whole planet.

And finally . . .

Scientists think there could be more than 50,000 spiders per 0.6 square mile (1 square kilometer) of land—on average. Some give another strange average. It is difficult to prove, but each human is thought to eat eight spiders in his or her lifetime. It happens as you sleep and a spider crawls across the pillow. . . . Just hope yours is not a bird-eating tarantula!

organ   part of the body that performs a particular job
vital   very important; essential

51

Find Out More

Website

Smithsonian Institute National Zoological Park
Website with articles, information, and many photos of all kinds of animals.
nationalzoo.si.edu

Books

Greenaway, Theresa. *Secret World of: Spiders*. Chicago: Raintree, 2003.

Llewellyn, Claire. *Minibeasts: Spiders*. Danbury, Conn.: Franklin Watts, 2000.

Otfinoski, Steven. *Spiders and Other Arachnids*. Chicago: World Book, 2001.

Steele, Christy. *Animals of the Rainforest: Tarantulas*. Chicago: Raintree, 2003.

World Wide Web

If you want to find out more about arachnids, you can search the Internet using keywords such as these:

- arachnid
- spiders + scorpions
- "red spider mites"

You can also find your own keywords by using headings or words from this book. Use the following search tips to help you find the most useful websites.

Search tips

There are billions of pages on the Internet, so it can be difficult to find exactly what you want to find. For example, if you just type in "water" on a search engine such as Google, you will get a list of millions webpages. These search skills will help you find useful websites more quickly:

- Use simple keywords instead of whole sentences.
- Use two to six keywords in a search, putting the most important words first.
- Be precise—only use names of people, places, or things.
- If you want to find words that go together, put quote marks around them.
- Use the advanced section of your search engine.
- Use the "+" sign between keywords to link them.

Where to search

Search engine
A search engine looks through a small proportion of the Web and lists all sites that match the words in the search box. It can give thousands of links, but the best matches are at the top of the list, on the first page. Try nationalzoo.si.edu/search

Search directory
A search directory is like a library of websites that have been sorted by a person instead of a computer. You can search by keyword or subject and browse through the different sites like you look through books on a library shelf.
A good example is yahooligans.com.

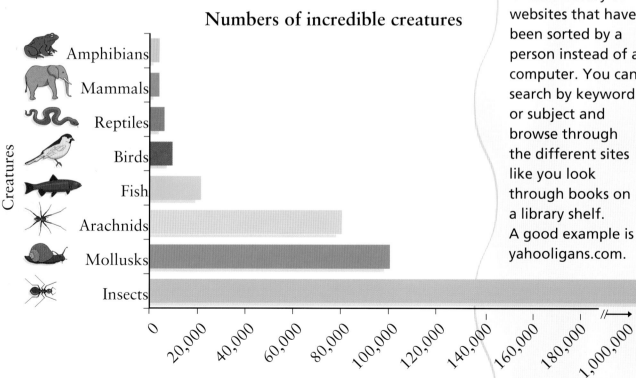

Numbers of incredible creatures

Creatures: Amphibians, Mammals, Reptiles, Birds, Fish, Arachnids, Mollusks, Insects

Number of species (approximate): 0, 20,000, 40,000, 60,000, 80,000, 100,000, 120,000, 140,000, 160,000, 180,000, 1,000,000

Glossary

abandon   give up and leave something behind

abdomen   part of the body containing the stomach (the rear part of a spider)

allergic   having a bad reaction, often involving sneezing, itching, or rashes

antennae   feelers on an insect's head

antidote   medicine to make a poison safe

antifreeze   liquid that does not freeze at temperatures below 32 °F (0 °C)

arachnophobia   fear of spiders

arthritis   painful disease affecting the joints of the body

arthropod   animal with jointed legs but no backbone

asthma   disease or allergic reaction that affects the lungs and breathing

blister   small bubble or swelling on the skin

burrow   hole made for shelter; also, to make such as hole

camouflage   color that matches the background

cannibal   animal that eats its own species

captivity   held in a cage or tank

carbon dioxide   gas that animals and humans breathe out

carnivore   animals that eat meat

cell   tiny building block that makes up all living things

climate   general weather conditions in an area over a period of time

cocoon   silky case for protection

crustacean   sea arthropod with a hard shell, such as a crab, shrimp, or lobster

customs   officers at a port, airport, or frontier who check for people who import things illegally

digestive juices   acid and fluid made in the stomach to break down food

disguise   change appearance to look different

disinfectant   liquid or ointment that kills germs

ecosystem   balance between all living things in their natural environment

egg sac   small case that holds an egg or eggs and food for the young to eat

endangered   in danger of dying out completely

exaggerated   made to sound like a bigger deal than it is; far-fetched

extinct   die out, never to return

fertilize   when a sperm joins an egg to make a new individual

filter   something that traps large bits

follicle   any small opening in the skin, such as a hair follicle

food chain   order in which one living thing feeds on another

fossil   very old remains of things that once lived, found in mud and rock

funnel   cone shape

gills   flaps on the sides of a fish's head used for breathing oxygen from water

gland   part of the body that makes chemicals and other substances

habitat   natural home of an animal

hibernate   "close down" the body to rest when it is too cold or dry

host   animal or plant that has a parasite living on it

illegal   against the law

immune system   body's natural defense against infection

import   bring into the country from another country

inhabitant   person who lives in a certain place

invertebrate   animal without a backbone

irregular   no organized pattern, shape, or design

larva   young form of an animal that is very different from the adult

leg span   distance between stretched-out legs

lethal   deadly

mammal   warm-blooded animal that has hair and feed its young with milk

mange   skin disease causing itching and loss of hair in animals

microscopic   can only be seen using an instrument that magnifies tiny objects

molt   lose skin or hair before new growth

nocturnal   active at night and not in the day

nutrient   important substance found in food and needed by the body

nymph   in-between stage from larva to adult

official record   information reported by the correct authority

organ   part of the body that performs a particular job

oxygen   one of the gases in air and water that all living things need

paralyze   stun a creature so it is unable to move

parasite   animal or plant that lives in or on another living thing

pedipalps   spider's two feelers, like short front legs; used for touching and tasting

pesticide   poison sprayed onto crops to kill insects

pierce   stab or break through a surface

pincer   hook at the front of some creatures' mouths for holding food

pollute   ruin natural things with dangerous chemicals, fumes, or garbage

predator   animal that hunts and eats other animals

prey   animal that is killed and eaten

protein   nutrient in food that is used by the body for growth and repair

rappel   descend from a height on a rope

regurgitate   throw up the contents of the stomach

remote   faraway place in the middle of nowhere

scabies   skin disease causing severe itching

segment   section

shed   get rid of an outer layer

specialize   focus on one thing and be skilled at it

species   type of living animal or plant

sperm   male sex cell

stalk   hunt down by following and creeping up on a victim

survive   stay alive despite dangers

swollen   puffed-up, enlarged

telson   last section of a scorpion's tail, with the venom sac at the end

thorax   part of the body between the head and abdomen; like a human's chest

thriving   growing with strength and doing very well

tissue   soft parts of the body; a collection of cells

tolerate   put up with something

toxic   poisonous

ultraviolet   invisible light from the sun

venom   poison

venomous   poisonous

vertical   going straight up, like a wall

vibration   quivering movement or fast shaking

victim   animal that gets hurt or killed

vital   very important, essential

Index